Teaching Your Child to Be Home Alone

Teaching Your Child to Be Home Alone

Earl A. Grollman
Gerri L. Sweder

LEXINGTON BOOKS
A Division of Macmillan, Inc.
New York

Maxwell Macmillan Canada
Toronto

Maxwell Macmillan International
New York   Oxford   Singapore   Sydney

Library of Congress Cataloging-in-Publication Data

Grollman, Earl A.
    Teaching your child to be home alone / Earl A. Grollman and
Gerri L. Sweder.
        p.   cm.
    ISBN 0-02-913135-9
    1. Latchkey children—United States.   2. Child rearing—United
States. I. Sweder, Gerri L. II. Title
HQ777.65.G76   1992
649′.1—dc20
                                                                92-19311
                                                                    CIP

Lexington Books
An Imprint of Macmillan, Inc.
866 Third Avenue, New York, N. Y. 10022

Maxwell Macmillan Canada, Inc.
1200 Eglinton Avenue East
Suite 200
Don Mills, Ontario M3C 3N1

Macmillan, Inc. is part of the Maxwell Communication Group of
Companies.

Printed in the United States of America

printing number
1   2   3   4   5   6   7   8   9   10

For Netta,
and our dear grandchildren,
Jennifer, Eric, Aaron, Sam, Rebecca, and Adam
Earl

For Ken
and our children,
who help us celebrate life,
Justin and Rebecca
Gerri

Always with Love

Contents

Contents

Contents

Introduction

Welcome. You are about to embark on a journey that is already being traveled by an estimated eight to ten million families whose children are home alone each weekday before and after school. This journey can be an adventure of growth and independence, as well as of increasing familial closeness and support. Being well prepared for this new challenge is crucial to ensure its success. Before you take off, it is important for you to consider these challenges: How can mothers and fathers determine when their children are ready to be unsupervised? Are children able to tell their parents when they are really scared? How can children understand their parents' feelings?

We wanted to know the answers to these questions—the questions so many parents are asking themselves. We have developed the stories in the following pages from our interviews and questionnaires with almost one thousand schoolchildren throughout the United States. They were eager to give advice so that others could learn from them.

We sat in classrooms and lunchrooms, in cities, suburbs, and small towns, with children who live with one or with two parents, listening, talking, and sharing ideas. We discussed youngsters' fears and heard tales of children who felt unprepared to meet the daily challenges of being on their own. Many adolescents whom we met expressed alarm at walking into an empty house every afternoon. Talking about their fears was a relief for them. Finding out that their classmates were also uneasy made them realize that their own feelings were not uncommon.

We also heard accounts of growth and change. Children spoke warmly of parents who helped and supported them in becoming more self-sufficient. These mothers and fathers offered their children guidance, love, and most important, a continued sensitivity to their feelings and needs.

We met with teachers and principals as well. Every day they see growing numbers of children who are home alone before and after school. They are concerned and troubled that too many young people are not being prepared for this major responsibility. They believe that too many parents assume that youngsters know more than they really do and are capable of more than they really are.

Teaching Your Child to Be Home Alone has been written to allay parents' sense of guilt and uncertainty, and to help children become more mindful of their parents' concerns. Chapter 1 is specifically devoted to helping youngsters develop a better understanding of what their working mothers and fathers are thinking about. Beginning in Chapter 2, we provide mothers and fathers with information about children's concerns, so that they can better know when a youngster is ready to be alone and for how long. An opportunity is created where mothers and fathers are able to express everyday worries.

This is a sharing book—it is intended for both parents and children to read and discuss, to improve communication between parents and children. Many youngsters admitted to us that they were reluctant to tell their parents of their anxieties, not wanting to increase their parents' uneasiness about leaving them on their own. By discussing the issues raised in this book, parents and children move through a step-by-step growth process to a greater independence, aware that dependence is also a strength. From better communicating with their children, mothers and fathers will be better prepared to make an informed decision in judging the ability, knowledge, and emotional readiness of their youngsters to be home alone.

Teaching Your Child to Be Home Alone is a valuable resource guide, filled with specific, practical advice. The narratives in these pages are the normal, everyday experiences that children home alone encounter. Some of the questions that youngsters told us they think about are:

"Why do I feel afraid being alone?"

"What should I do in case of an emergency?"

"How do I keep myself busy all afternoon?"

"Why do my parents worry so much about me?"

Parents, for their part, have their own considerations:

"Have I fully prepared my youngster to be home alone?"

"Do my children know how much I appreciate their growing independence?"

"Is my child showing signs of stress?"

You might want to read the stories together with your children. Talk about the issues. Remember that each youngster in your family will have a particular reaction to being alone, just as each parent will respond differently to this new stage of development.

Don't rush. Start at the beginning. Learning takes time, after all. Some families may need to focus on their own most pressing issues, then explore those areas that they have omitted later. With honest communication comes an appreciation of a youngster's abilities; with acceptance comes the strength to build upon an increased self-awareness.

Your children may be embarrassed by their own lack of information. Explain to them that youngsters are not expected to have all the answers. That is why you are reading this book with them. Be particularly sensitive not only to what they say but how they say it. Be conscious of their emotional reactions. Children left alone at too early an age or who are unprepared for such an experience often show signs of tension and stress, such as poor school performance, stomachaches, difficulty falling asleep, and aggressive or withdrawing behavior.

Communication works both ways. Just as mothers and fathers develop a deeper understanding of their children as they work on this issue together, youngsters gain fresh insights and appreciation of how hard their parents are trying to balance family and work life.

Each topic in each chapter in *Teaching Your Child to Be Home Alone* is divided into two parts. The first part consists of an anecdote related to a subject that we heard during our interviews. The range of topics illustrates how many children and parents feel and what they need to learn about each other. Children may not realize what it is like for a parent to return to a messy house after a hard day's work. Or they may understand that they are never to tell a stranger at the door that they are by themselves, but they may still be troubled by telling an untruth. Level of knowledge is not the only criterion in deciding a child's readiness to be unsupervised. Children may know they are supposed to call their mother or father when they return from school, but their frequent forgetfulness may be a sign that they are not yet ready for this new undertaking.

After parents and youngsters respond to the questions following the story, they may turn to the section in each topic's discussion called "Thinking Ahead." In our nation-wide study, we found *most* children are less prepared than mothers and fathers realize. Although parents may believe their children are capable of handling frightening situations or the loneliness of being by themselves, these expectations may differ greatly from the reality. The "Thinking Ahead" sections will help parents and children discover where the gaps lie and what needs to be filled in before children feel prepared to stay alone.

The "Talking it Out" section that follows in each topic discussion focuses on the psychological reactions to enable parents and children to become more aware of each other's needs. Parents are concerned about their children's ability to cope emotionally with the daily experience of being alone and the unexpected crises that might arise. "Talking it Out" highlights what youngsters need most—sympathetic responses and caring concern when they are frightened or feeling insecure. These sections will help mothers and fathers become more attuned to signs of stress and respond to them quickly and appropriately. The process of preparing children to stay in an unsupervised setting requires emotional maturity and learning competency.

The final chapter in the book is called "Testing Yourself." Our "Readiness Scale" allows mothers and fathers to score their children's responses to twenty-five key questions to determine whether the children are ready to be home alone. From our research we also developed a "Communication Scale," recognizing that children who have loving, supportive relationships with their mothers or fathers cope more readily in unsupervised settings. Finally, the "Child's Thoughts" section provide space for further reflection, a place where kids are able to express their lingering fears or doubts, hopes and expectations.

Make the most of your time together. There is much for you to think about and talk about with your children. Being home alone can be a wonderful growth experience for children who are prepared for it. Kids may delight in being on their own, with the sense of independence and freedom it brings. They may be challenged to solve problems and feel good about their newly acquired abilities. They will likely develop a level of responsibility with an increased sense of competence. They will learn to make creative use of time and reasoned choices. They see themselves as confident young people with mothers and fathers who are supportive and appreciative.

We would love to hear from you about your own experiences with these issues. What other situations, ideas, or suggestions do you think should be included in our next edition of *Teaching Your Child to Be Home Alone*? Please write to us at 2 Concord Avenue, Belmont, Massachusetts 02178. We, too, are always interested in learning.

The Survey and Interviews

The students we spoke with and those who answered a special questionnaire came from various socioeconomic and ethnic backgrounds. They lived in all parts of the country and were drawn from a sampling of twenty school districts in eleven states. These youngsters attended public, private, and parochial schools, and were in grades four, six, eight, ten, and twelve. They were from cities, suburbs, and rural areas. Our research combined a specifically prepared Survey of Attitudes as well as in-person interviews.

The written survey was anonymous, lasting forty minutes. Six-hundred forty-one students responded. Fifty-six percent of those answering were female; forty-four percent were male. Included in this survey were several standardized psychological tests, including Coopersmith Self-Esteem Inventories and Hollander Parent Contact Scale.

Additionally, we conducted in-depth oral interviews with almost four-hundred school-aged youngsters in both large and small groups. Whether spoken or written down, the sentiments, feelings, and suggestions of these studens clearly reflect concern that too many youngsters are left unprepared, uneducated, and afraid. It is our hope and wish that *Teaching Your Child to Be Home Alone* will prepare, educate, and allay fear for both parent and child as they meet this new challenge together.

Starting Out

This easy to use, practical guide needs only a few instructions. *Teaching Your Child to Be Home Alone* allows mothers and fathers to help their children learn the basics of: personal safety, coping with loneliness and fear, using time creatively, and responding quickly and thoughtfully to emergencies. On the other hand, *Teaching Your Child to Be Home Alone* enables children to better understand why parents worry when a youngster doesn't call, are upset when they return to a messy house, and feel anxious about leaving their daughter or son alone before and after school.

How to begin? There are many ways to use this book. One suggestion is to sit down with your child and read the stories together to best determine what your youngster knows and what is not known. Others may prefer that child and parent read separately, coming together later to discuss what has been learned and what questions need answering. You may discover that the anecdotes sound familiar, as these reflect situations that can occur in almost all families.

Each "Thinking Ahead" section gives you the opportunity to teach and review; there is much to master. Each "Talking it Out" section allows you to open up dialogue; there are many feelings to be shared. Near the back of the book, the Readiness Scale gives both you and your child a means to determine if and when your child is ready and able to be home alone.

Chapter 1

Parental Concerns
about Children

Leaving for Work

It is 7:30 A.M., and Mr. and Mrs. Ying have to leave for work. Their ten-year-old son, Ben, does not have to be at school until an hour later.

They don't like to leave Ben home alone. They know that as soon as they close the door, he will turn on the television. They are concerned that one day Ben will become so engrossed in a TV program that he will forget to take his lunch or leave for school on time.

What could Mr. and Mrs. Ying do to help ease their minds in the mornings?

THINKING AHEAD

- Parents may feel uncomfortable leaving you alone when they depart for work.

- If you do feel capable of being alone, reassure your parents of your ability to handle this responsibility.

- Whenever possible, try to have breakfast with your mom or dad. Your parents want to connect with you.

- Try not to argue with your parents in the morning. You may forget about a dispute by the time first period begins, but chances are it will upset your mom or dad for a good portion of the day.

- Find out if there is a before-school drop-in program at your school.

- Your mom or dad might feel better if a friend joins you before class. Explore if there are classmates of yours in similar circumstances who would like company in the morning.

- Don't go to school early just because you don't like staying home alone. Teachers are busy preparing for the day, and they are not expected to care for youngsters until school officially begins.

TALKING IT OUT

Most adults report to work at a specific time each day. Mothers and fathers whose youngsters are still home while they are commuting to work may have an aching feeling of uncertainty. They may feel guilty because they are not around when they think they should be. Parents who must already be on the job before their children leave for school could call home to wish their children a good day and to make sure they are ready to leave. Most parents feel better after speaking with their children and thereby, reassuring themselves that all is well.

Parents worry about everything that could go wrong in the morning. They may be concerned that their children will forget their homework or their keys or be followed by a dog. They feel helpless because they are not nearby to respond.

Mothers and fathers can provide a secure environment

in the morning even though they cannot be home. They should explore all the options offered at school, in the neighborhood, or with their friends. Perhaps a neighbor who lives nearby could watch a group of youngsters whose parents must be at work early. Or the parents may be able to rearrange their work schedules so that one parent is able to be home for a longer time in the morning. If the children are prepared and willing, they could be left alone for a short period of time. By the time most youngsters reach sixth grade, they are able to get themselves ready for school.

The Three O'clock Dilemma

Chantal's mother, Susan, is a worrier. Susan went back to work three years ago, when Chantal was eight years old, and she enrolled Chantal in an after-school program. Chantal liked being with other kids when she was younger, and she knew her mom felt better because there were grownups at the program to take care of her. Now, at eleven, Chantal feels it's time for a change. She no longer wants to go to the program. She wants to be home in her own space. She decides to ask her mom what she is concerned about so that perhaps she can come home after school from now on.

Why do you think parents feel anxious when their children are home unsupervised?

What do you think would disturb your mom or dad if you were home by yourself?

THINKING AHEAD

- Parents worry about your being unsupervised whether or not you think there is a reason to be concerned.

- Set aside a time to talk about your parents' feelings. Respect what they share with you, and respond to their concerns.

- Your responsible behavior will help your parents feel more at ease about your being home alone. Do you return home at the agreed-upon time every day? Are you aware of safety precautions and do you take those precautions? Do you know how to respond to strangers on the phone or at the door? Can you entertain yourself in other ways than by watching television?

- Your parents will feel better when they can speak with you during the day to find out that you are safe and occupied.

TALKING IT OUT

Because mothers and fathers love their children, parents worry about something happening to their children when they are at work and are unable to offer immediate assistance. They wonder whether they have adequately prepared their children to be by themselves. Parents have real concerns about matters they cannot control, such as a stranger approaching their children as they walk home from school, or their children cutting themselves as they slice a sandwich.

When parents share their fears and feelings about their youngsters' well-being, their children are better able to respond to specific, legitimate parental concerns. Children cannot keep their mothers and fathers from being anxious about them, any more than parents can prevent their youngsters from being concerned when they are late. People worry because they care. That is all the reason they need.

Child Forgets to Call

As soon as Sharon comes home from school at 3:35 P.M., she is supposed to call her mother at work to tell her that she's arrived safely. But now it's 4:15 P.M., and Mrs. Gluck hasn't heard a word from her daughter. She tries to remember if Sharon told her if she was going somewhere after school. She calls Sharon's friend Elizabeth, but Elizabeth says she hasn't seen Sharon since gym class that morning. Now Mrs. Gluck is getting very worried. She telephones her house, then her neighbor. Still there is no word of Sharon.

What should Mrs. Gluck do?

Have you ever forgotten to call a parent? If so, what was the reaction?

What would you do if you tried to reach your mother or father and couldn't?

THINKING AHEAD

- Be sure to call your parents at the scheduled time so that they will not worry.

- If you know beforehand that you will be somewhere without a telephone, tell your parents where you will be and what time you will be home.

- Write down your daily after-school activities, and make sure at least one of your parents has a copy.

- Give your parents the phone numbers of your close friends, so that they can call them if they have not heard from you.

Name_____

Phone Number_____

Name_____

Phone Number_____

Name_____

Phone Number_____

- When you call one of your parents but they are not available, leave a message to say that you phoned, the time of day, where you are, and how you may be reached later.

TALKING IT OUT

Mothers and fathers are naturally concerned if they don't hear from their children at the designated time. It is the children's commitment to contact their parents. Doing so demonstrates that they are mature and dependable. Even though youngsters may feel that they are too old to have to telephone their mother or father, it is simply one of those things children have to do. Parents are natural worriers. A telephone call will ease their anxiety.

Illness

Mrs. Garcia is busy at work preparing a report. The telephone rings, and the school nurse tells her that her ten-year-old son, Gabriel, is feeling ill and running a fever of 102° Fahrenheit. Mrs. Garcia calls her husband, but he is out of the office. She informs her boss that she needs to leave, then quickly gathers her materials so that she can work at home.

What do you think is going through Mrs. Garcia's mind?

Has this situation ever happened in your family? If so, what did you do?

THINKING AHEAD

- At some time, your parents will probably be called at work because you are ill.

- Physicians recommend that you remain home if you have any of the following symptoms:

  - a fever of 100°F (38°C) or higher

  - vomiting

  - diarrhea and abdominal pain

  - generally feeling unwell.

- Develop with your parents a list of people they can call in case an emergency arises and neither one of them can easily leave work. The school should be given this list as well.

Name _____

Phone number _____

Relationship to child (grandfather, friend, neighbor) ___

_____

Name _____

Phone number _____

Relationship to child (grandfather, friend, neighbor) ___

_____

- If you develop a pattern of going to the nurse for stomachaches or undiagnosed complaints, you may have to be tested for a possible underlying problem. Signs of stress or distress often show up as physical symptoms.

TALKING IT OUT

Children, like adults, feel especially vulnerable and are in need of extra nurturing when they don't feel well. They do not want to sit in a nurse's office all day; nor do they want to be left home alone. Often the best medicine is a sympathetic parent or caregiver with lots of extra attention.

When parents receive an unexpected call from a school nurse, they have no control over the reactions of their supervisors or colleagues. Parents wish their jobs were flexible enough that they can easily leave in an emergency. Mothers and fathers are also aware that when they return to work after an emergency, the volume of work that has piled up in their absence may well be burdensome. They may have to subtract the number of days they spent at home from their vacation time or their own sick days. They may even worry that they could lose their position. While leaving work in the middle of the day is obviously disruptive to business, too few employers appreciate the terrible dilemmas that families face when a youngster is ill.

When mothers and fathers share the responsibility of caring for a sick child, there is less pressure. Parents can juggle their schedules, while children will have to recognize that it may be necessary for their parents to conduct business on the phone at home or complete an assignment there. Youngsters who are sick can sleep, read a book, or watch a videotape while their parent works. Being prepared for a child's illness can lessen the sense of tension, especially if the youngster must stay home from school for several days.

A Messy House

Mrs. Waldman arrives home from work at 6:15 P.M., but she is not prepared for what she is about to see. Jackets and book bags are lying on the floor. The kitchen counter is piled with dirty dishes. Food is sitting out on the table.

"Josh," Mrs. Waldman calls out to her son. "I want to speak to you—now!" As soon as Mrs. Waldman sees Josh, she shouts, "Look at this place! It's disgusting! I can't stand coming home to such a mess after working all day. You know you're supposed to clean up after yourself and your friends!"

"It's no big deal!" Josh hollers back. "I'll clean it up later. I don't know why you're so angry!"

How do you think Mrs. Waldman is feeling right now?

Have similar situations occurred within your family? If so, how did each of you react?

THINKING AHEAD

- No one should have to clean up after you.

- Get into the habit of putting your things away when you come home from school. Hang up your jacket, deposit your books in one place, and make sure your dirty clothes go into the laundry bag.

- Your friends should help you clean up any mess they have made at your house. Remember, you are responsible for their actions.

- There will probably be consequences for you if your parents return to an untidy home. You could lose some of your privileges.

TALKING IT OUT

It's hard for parents to work all day long, then return to a messy home. Adults often need orderliness, especially at the end of the day. Mothers and fathers should make it clear to their children that they expect them to assume the responsibility for cleaning up after themselves and their guests.

Children, like adults, have good and bad days alike. Parents understand that occasionally youngsters forget to tidy up. But if this becomes a pattern, mothers and fathers feel let down. It means they still have a lot to do that evening. Most important, parents want to be able to spend time with their children, not have to pick up after them.

In order for their household to run more smoothly, family members need to show consideration for one another. Youngsters can demonstrate their appreciation of their parents' efforts by trying to adhere to parental standards. Mothers and fathers should not expect perfection, but they can expect their children to be thoughtful.

Picking Up Children at the End of the Day

Mr. McCarthy has had a tough day. His former wife called to complain about a personal problem she was having. This made him so upset that he had

*an argument with a co-worker about a trivial
matter. Now it is 5:30 P.M., and he leaves work to
pick up his son at the after-school program.*

*When Mr. McCarthy arrives, Simon is busy
playing Monopoly with his friends Carlos and Tyler.
Mr. McCarthy wants Simon to stop the game,
gather his belongings, and leave. But Simon isn't
ready—he wants another ten minutes to finish the
game.*

*Mr. McCarthy snaps, "I'll give you three minutes,
then we go!" Simon throws down the dice, grabs his
backpack, and runs down the stairs.*

What do you think happens next?

Have you had a similar experience? If so, how did you and
your family work it through?

THINKING AHEAD

- The end of the working day can be a difficult time
  for adults. It is natural for them to sometimes be
  tired and irritable.

- The end of the day can be difficult for you as well.
  You have spent a full day at school and extra hours
  in after-school care. It's natural for you to
  sometimes be tired and irritable.

- If you act grumpy, say you're sorry.

- Forgive each other when you say things you may
  regret later.

14

- Before your parent arrives at the center begin to get ready and be prepared to say good-bye to your friends so that pickup time is easier for everybody.

- Occasionally, you may be so involved in an activity that you are not quite prepared to leave an after-school program when your parents come to pick you up. Explain that you just need a few more minutes. Show what you are doing. Your mom or dad may decide to use this time to speak with your teacher.

- Don't make a habit of asking for additional time—your parent wants to go home.

Talking it Out

Many parents deeply wish they could be home from work when their children return at the end of the school day. But unfortunately, this is generally not possible. So parents do the next best thing—they arrange for their youngsters to be in a safe, caring environment with children their own age. Just knowing that their youngsters are in an adult-supervised setting helps parents feel more secure and better able to concentrate on their work.

After-school care is often exhilarating. Certainly, some days it can feel confining and exhausting too. There may be too much stimulation when a youngster needs a quiet place to wind down.

For parents, work can be challenging, but there are also times when nothing seems to go right: a co-worker becomes ill and the parent has to miss lunch to fill in; an expected shipment does not arrive; an important client decides to do business elsewhere. Traffic congestion going to and from work further frazzles parents' nerves.

For mothers and fathers—especially single parents—the second part of their day is about to begin as they leave the workplace. Parents want to be loving and responsive when they greet their children, and they feel bad when they snap and lose their temper. They realize that their children, especially at this moment, need loving caring and undistracted attention.

Transitions are difficult for children to make as well. Something might have occurred in school or day care that was upsetting to them. They may be feeling especially tired, have had an argument with a friend, or have received a low grade on a test. On the other hand, the day could have been exciting for them—being chosen for the soccer team, feeling relieved after doing an oral report, receiving an invitation to a party. Then the parent arrives just when the youngster is involved in an activity and is not quite ready to leave.

Some children fall apart when their parents arrive. The many hours they have spent in school and supervised care can be a strain. They keep themselves together, and when the parent appears, their bottled-up emotions are released in a flood. Such behavior upsets an already overwhelmed parent. If their child seems to have a hard time at the end of the day, parents could ask a teacher or caregiver to help the child wind down before being picked up.

Though parents and children often are both exhausted at the end of the day, they also look forward to being together. Angry words may sometimes be spoken, but mostly love and joy are expressed.

Returning to the Workforce

It has been three months since Mrs. Pollner returned to work as a dental hygienist. She arranges for six-year-old Kaitlin and eight-year-old Lindsay to stay with a neighbor after school while she is at work. Her oldest child, Scott, is a junior in high school and works after school.

Mrs. Pollner is exhausted. After she returns home from her job, she must clean and cook and help the younger children with their homework. Her family needs the money from her income, especially since Scott will be going to college in two years. She just wishes she could be home with Kaitlin and Lindsay, as she was with Scott.

What do you think some of Mrs. Pollner's feelings are?

Do you know anybody in a similar situation?

THINKING AHEAD

- Like you, most school-age children have parents in the workforce.

- Your parents may experience a lot of stress in entering or returning to the job market. It is difficult for them to balance work and family life.

- Give your mom and dad an unexpected hug or words of praise. Let them know what a good job they are doing.

- Ask your parents how you can help out. They will be grateful for your consideration. Sharing dinner preparation, for example, is a way to learn responsibility and be with one another at the same time.

- Fill out this weekly helping schedule.

Weekly Helping Schedule

Some ideas as to how you can help out around the house:

Organize your homework

Set the table

Make a salad

Empty the dishwasher

Clean up after dinner

Make your bed

Walk the dog

Take out the trash (or recycle it)

Fold the laundry

Other _____

TALKING IT OUT

Returning to the workplace can be a painful decision to make, especially for parents of younger children. Parents worry about how their youngsters will fare in the child care setting. Parents of older youngsters are concerned about how well their children will do on their own. Parents of adolescents have increasing apprehension levels because of the possible risks in their teenager's free-time activities without an adult presence.

It takes time for working parents to feel they are successfully balancing their home and work lives. Family members can help speed up this process. They can offer to contribute more to the daily running of the household, such as keeping their rooms neater. Youngsters can show support in other significant ways as well. They can tell their mothers that they are proud of them for taking on this new challenge, they can ask about their mother's work day, and they can argue somewhat less and listen somewhat more.

When parents join or reenter the job market, they may have concerns about their own competence. Their everyday performance is being evaluated by a supervisor or colleague. In addition, deadlines and other pressures may be imposed on them, all while they have to adhere to a company schedule not of their making.

Chapter 2

Children's Concerns

Loneliness

Danielle is not like many of her friends, who enjoy being home without supervision. It makes Danielle unhappy to be all alone, but she is too embarrassed to tell anyone how she feels. Only her diary knows how hard it is for her to stay by herself.

Her friend Helen still has someone take care of her in the afternoon. Danielle wishes that she were that lucky.

Do you know anyone who feels the way Danielle does?

Have you ever felt this way?

If so, what helps you when you feel uneasy?

THINKING AHEAD

- Many children your age do not want to be home by themselves.

- If You Are Afraid To Be Home Alone, Tell Your Parents. They care about you. Most mothers and fathers will listen readily, respect your feelings, and show understanding for what you are saying.

- Decide if you are uneasy about being by yourself all the time or just for certain periods of time. You might not mind being home while it's light out but get frightened when it becomes dark. You may enjoy staying alone for about an hour but no longer, or for two days but not five.

- If you do not feel ready to be alone, your parents should make every effort to place you in a supervised setting. Your parents could ask a grandparent, employ a high school or college student, find an after-school care program, or explore other resources in the community. Creative planning is necessary to meet your needs to be with others while your parents are at work.

If I were lonely and didn't want to be by myself, I would tell:

my mother

my father

a grandparent

a brother or sister

a friend

a teacher

other_____

I would probably rather be at _____ in the afternoon than be alone:

my friend's

my neighbor's house

an after-school program

a community center

a library

other _____

I think I would feel happier being on my own if:

my neighborhood were safer

there were other people around in the afternoon

my mother or father didn't come home so late

I had a pet to keep me company

I could have friends over

my parent called me each afternoon to talk

other _____

TALKING IT OUT

Most older children are able to successfully be home unsupervised. They enjoy the independence and freedom this brings. They can create their own schedule, be as loud as they like, or relish the hours of solitude. These older children are emotionally and mentally prepared for the experience of being home alone.

But other children feel pressured when they have to be alone. They are not yet ready to handle the tremendous responsibility of caring for themselves every afternoon. They are frightened and lonely. Many such children have told us that they feel rejected and angry, insecure—even abandoned. As a result of our research, we know that these children are at psychological risk. Many such youngsters told us that their parents do not understand how upset they are.

Through our surveys and interviews, we have found that *children age twelve and younger who were regularly left home alone for two hours or more scored significantly lower on tests measuring self-esteem* than did their peers who were home alone only one hour or less. These children reported having problems in their ability to communicate with their parents, a lower degree of self-confidence, and poorer school performance. Teachers, principals, and guidance counselors agree with this assessment and speak of the gradual increase in the number of children in their classrooms who are needy of nurturance because they are alone for too long and feel vulnerable.

Some children react to stressful situations by becoming withdrawn or aggressive. Their school grades drop, or they have trouble sleeping or are tired much of the time. Many develop health-related problems, such as frequent stomachaches or headaches. Mothers and fathers should be alert to changes of behavior in their children and be prepared to respond quickly, lovingly, and responsively.

Youngsters should not be intimidated or bribed to stay home by themselves; nor should they be made to feel that they are immature or failing the parent if they share their anxieties with them. Parents should avoid making comparisons between their children and other people's children, for each youngster is different. Some need more guidance, self-confidence, and support than others in order to cope with new situations.

Unfortunately, finding good after-school care is difficult —at best. Many phone calls have to be made, sites visited, centers' reputations checked out—all time-consuming projects. We have great empathy for parents who are trying to provide the best for themselves and their children.

Darkness

Eric, a fifth grader, really likes to be home alone after school during the day. He works on his models, plays around with the computer, and has the dog all to himself. But when it starts to get dark, his apartment begins to seem a bit creepy to him. He suddenly pays special attention to strange noises outside in the hall. He dosen't feel safe until his brother Jeremy gets home.

Why do you think Eric feels this way?

Have you ever been home alone when it is dark outside? How did you feel?

Have you shared your feelings with your mom or dad?

THINKING AHEAD

- Before it gets dark, turn on the lights. That way you will feel more comfortable moving from room to room.

- Identify those areas of your apartment or house that feel the creepiest to you in the dark. Go into those

areas in the light. Make those areas easier to enter
at night by placing an extra lamp there.

- If you avoid a room because it feels scary in the
  dark, tell your parent that you feel frightened. Let
  them help you take control of your fear.

- Remember, space itself is neither alarming or
  soothing. Shadows that are cast on a floor or wall
  look different in darkness from the way they look in
  the daytime. It is how you see a space that matters.

- Turning on the radio or television can help.

- Find out which of your friends are home alone too.
  Call them when it gets darker, so you can help each
  other feel more relaxed.

- If your house is relatively unlit or isolated, ask your
  parents to consider installing outdoor floodlights for
  your peace of mind.

- If you live in an apartment building where lights are
  burned out in the hallway or stairs, ask your parents
  to have these replaced or to replace them
  themselves.

TALKING IT OUT

Some children want to be by themselves when it is light
outside, but they need an older person or a friend to stay
with them later in the day. If their youngster seems anxious
about being alone when it is dark, parents should discuss
ways of lessening those fears. One approach may be for a

parent or grandparent to call to say hi and check on how the youngster is doing. Hobbies should be encouraged as a means of fun and distraction. Parents and children could select appropriate television viewing for this time period and avoid scary programs. If this does not seem to be sufficient, parents could look into arranging for dark-time supervision. Remember—many adults, too, feel more fearful in the dark.

Calling a Parent at Work

As he walks home from school each afternoon, ten-year-old David thinks about what he is going to tell his father when he calls him. Today, Friday, he wants to know if his friend Yeah-Juin can sleep over and if his father will pick up a video for them on his way home from work.

David feels good about calling his dad each day. He knows his father loves to hear what is happening to him—even the bad time, such as when he forgot to bring in his map and the teacher made him stay in from recess.

How do you think David might feel if he could not call his father after school?

Do you speak to either of your parents when you come home from school? If so, what kinds of things do you share together?

Is this helpful to you? Why?

THINKING AHEAD

- Write down your mother's and father's work numbers.

- If possible, decide on a time when you can call your parents each day so as not to disrupt their work schedule. Your mother and father might alternate times so that both have an opportunity to stay in touch with you when they are at work.

- Your parents may need to set guidelines concerning the number of calls and the duration of those calls. This is because your parent may be able to speak to you for only a few minutes.

- If your call concerns an *emergency*, state that clearly and quickly so that your parent can *immediately* be summoned to the phone.

- During times when your parents are unable to receive incoming calls, they may arrange for a time when they can phone you.

- If neither of your parents can receive or make calls, they should consider designating a responsible adult to be your "phone mate." This phone mate should be someone you like, such as a grandparent or a close friend's parent.

- Fill out this Weekly Phone chart.

Weekly Phone Chart

Write down whom you are to call each afternoon to tell that you are home and safe.

MON	TUES	WED	THURS	FRI

TALKING IT OUT

Whether parents call their children themselves or arrange for their children to phone them, daily contact is crucial. Youngsters want to know that their mothers or fathers are thinking of them at work. Youngsters told us in our interviews that on their way home from school, they often rehearse in their minds what they wish to tell their parents.

Our research also shows that 60 percent of mothers and 45 percent of fathers sometimes call home. Unfortunately, we found that youngsters who are left alone the longest have parents who call them the most infrequently. Fewer than half the mothers and only one-third of the fathers telephone these youngsters on a regular basis. We found that these children generally have lower self-esteem, have greater adjustment problems, and feel more isolated than their peers who enjoy regular phone contact with parents. These parents seem to be less in tune with their youngsters' emotional needs.

A parent's voice on the other end of the telephone eases the child's transition from the crowded classroom to the quiet house. Children want their parents to know that they have arrived home safely, and they hope their parents look forward to knowing about their school day. Parents are the most important people in a child's life to rejoice in the good grade on the science exam or in being chosen for the team.

Mothers and fathers also supply emotional support when children are frightened or need to share a problem. Children often need immediate release and recognition of their feelings. They want understanding and sympathy, especially if their day has gone badly.

Telephoning also has practical purposes. Parents can inform their child about a schedule change that would alter their expected arrival home, give the child instructions about starting dinner, or discuss a difficult homework question.

A phone call allows parents and children to say to each other "I miss you" and "I love you." Disagreements should be delayed until parents and youngsters are able to sit down together face to face. Children crave reassurance, and they look forward to conversations that are warm and affectionate. Parents, for their part, feel better when they spend a few loving minutes "visiting" on the phone with their youngster.

A Parent Is Late

Sarah is accustomed to her mother coming home by 5:30 P.M. every day. Her older sister Jessie doesn't arrive home from her job at the mall until 7:00 P.M. Sarah likes to spend this time alone with her mother without having to compete with Jessie. They talk and share stories about their day. Sarah sets the table and sits down in the kitchen while her mom makes dinner. By the time Jessie comes home, supper is ready. Then they all sit down to eat together.

But tonight is different. It is ten of six, and Sarah's mother still isn't home. Sarah is getting a queasy feeling. She keeps staring at the clock. By 6:05, she is terribly anxious. She turns on the television, but it doesn't help. Sarah takes out a box of cookies and pops one after another into her mouth.

What do you think Sarah is thinking?

What should Sarah do?

Has your mom or dad sometimes been much later than expected in coming home from work? If so, how did you react?

THINKING AHEAD

- Your parents should always call home if they are going to leave work later than expected, even if they will be delayed for only a short time.

- Their places of business, office telephone numbers, and addresses should be written down and easily accessible to you.

33

- If your parents cannot reach you because the phone is busy or you have not returned from an after-school activity, they could call and ask a relative, friend, or neighbor to inform you of their delay.

- As a daily reminder, your mother or father could mark any change of routine on a bulletin board or anyplace else where notes are kept. Telling you casually in the morning as they rush out the door is not sufficient because it's so easy to forget. Instructions should be specific, such as "I will not be home until 6:30 tonight because I have a haircut appointment at Helen's. Her phone number is_____."

- Work out with your parents a plan of action for what you will do in case they are delayed. For example, you could listen to a radio station that broadcasts reports of traffic and public transportation delays. Check the bulletin board to see if your mother or father planned to stop off at a particular place before returning home, such as the supermarket or the cleaners.

- Have the phone numbers of people to call when you are worried. If you are very upset about being alone, know at least one home where you can wait for your parent or parents to return. If you go to another place, leave a note informing your parents where you will be. Don't leave the note on the front door. Tape it to the refrigerator or any other conspicuous spot.

- If my mom or dad is late, I can call:

Name _____

Phone Number _____

Name _____

Phone Number _____

Name _____

Phone Number _____

TALKING IT OUT

When parents are late in returning from work, children become frightened. Often, parents are detained through no fault of their own. Still, many children told us they panic. One of the greatest fears children harbor is that harm will come to their parents. What may seem like a short delay to parents is a very long absence for children. These children need reassurance and comfort, as well as an explanation for the reason why their parents were not home on time. Children are concerned. Accidents do occur. Youngsters' anxieties and anger are normal reactions to their fears.

When parents accept their children's upset feelings, it helps their children understand the importance of their own responsibility to call their parents when they are tardy in returning home from school or any other activity.

Chapter 3

Preparing for the Unexpected

Noises

Eleven-year-old Thea is upstairs in her room. She has been home from school for almost an hour, and she is absorbed in a book. Her sisters, Lara and Alexandra, are not due home from field hockey practice for another hour.

Thea hears a strange noise downstairs. Her heart starts to pound. She strains to hear if the sound returns. Even the sound of her own breathing seems louder. She hears the noise again. It sounds like a tapping against a window. She wonders if she should go downstairs and check out the noise.

What do you think Thea should do?

Has anything like this ever happened to you? If so, what did you do?

THINKING AHEAD

- Most important, if you are frightened for any reason, call a parent, neighbor, or friend.

- Pay attention to the special noises where you live. Each apartment or house has its unique sounds. You may be so used to these sounds when there are other people around that you do not "hear" them, but when you are home alone, noises seem louder and more alarming.

• With your mom or dad, try sitting silently in different places in your home. Listen for sounds. What sounds occur again and again? You might want to pay special attention to the heater or air conditioner clicking on and off, to traffic noises, or to the elevator door opening and closing.

• When you are alone and hear a strange sound, think about the possible reasons for the noise. Is it the wind, or is it the refrigerator or the cat? If you decide it's nothing scary or dangerous, try to ignore it. Distract yourself by turning on the radio or television.

• If you cannot figure out what is causing the scary sound, call and ask a neighbor to come over and check out the noise. Have the telephone numbers of people you could call in the afternoon in case of such an emergency. This person(s) can be your safety checker.

My first safety checker is _____

Phone Number _____

My second safety checker is _____

Phone Number _____

TALKING IT OUT

Everyone is frightened by sudden noises. When people are absorbed in their own thoughts or activities, they tend to block out many of the sounds around them. But when there is a loud or unexpected noise, their whole body responds—especially if they are children home alone. Their tense reactions are a natural response to possible danger: they arouse them to become more alert to what is going on around them, and they prepare them to take action if necessary. Most noises youngsters hear are ordinary, every-day sounds. Children may be jarred for the moment, but they should be able to resume normal activity once the source of the sound has been identified. Yet not all sounds are harmless.

Youngsters need to know that when they need comforting, they should call someone who can offer them reassurance. Mothers and fathers should understand that when a fear is shared, children are less afraid. When youngsters are unable to talk about upsetting situations or work out satisfactory solutions to them, they may show signs of underlying anxiety and stress.

The most helpful message a parent can give their anxious youngster: "I will always listen and help the best way I can."

A Stranger at the Door

Soon after Lauren, age ten, comes home from school, her doorbell rings. She hopes that it's her friend Katie. Instead, there is a man in a delivery uniform. He tells her he has a package for her father and asks her to sign for it.

Lauren opens the door for the man, takes the package, and signs her father's name. When the man drives away, Lauren wonders whether she did the right thing.

What would you do if you were by yourself and a stranger knocked at the door?

What would you do if an unfamiliar person insisted on speaking to your parent?

THINKING AHEAD

- *Never open the door for someone you don't know.*

- Do not admit to any stranger that you are home alone. You could say, "My mother cannot come to the door right now, but she asked if you could come back at another time," or, "My dad cannot be disturbed, so please leave the package on the steps."

- Before you open the door, always ask who it is. Even if you are expecting a friend, an unfamiliar person could be there. Your parents could install a peephole so you will know who is outside the door.

- There are many reasons why strangers come to your door. They may be interested in having someone sign a petition, donate money to a cause, or purchase a magazine subscription. They may be lost and need directions, have a car that has broken down, or be at the wrong house. Still, you do not open the door no matter how needy or nice a person sounds.

- The fact that a person is in a delivery uniform or even a police uniform is no guarantee that that person can be trusted. People can impersonate even law enforcement officers.

- If you feel threatened, call a neighbor or your parents.

TALKING IT OUT

It can be very frightening for children alone to hear the doorbell and see an unfamiliar face. It's impossible to know whether the person has come on a simple errand. Most people who come to a house are just carrying out their jobs and will never harm anyone. But youngsters must always be extra cautious.

Mothers and fathers should talk with their children about those people who can be trusted and those to be wary of. Parents should not arrange for repair services to be performed when a child is home alone. Expecting a child to let in one particular stranger is asking too much and could prove dangerous.

It's too bad that parents and children cannot readily trust everyone who knocks at the door and that sometimes kids have to tell an untruth for safety purposes. But a closed door provides the necessary measure of protection for the peace of mind of both parents and children.

A Stranger Telephones

Ten-year-old Adam has just plopped down on the living-room couch to rest and watch some television before his mom comes home from work. The ring of the telephone startles him. When Adam answers, a man on the other end asks to speak to his mother. Adam tells the man that his mom is busy and can't come to the phone. The man on the other end says he will wait for her until she is available.

What should Adam do?

How do you think Adam is feeling right now?

THINKING AHEAD

- Most children are uncomfortable when someone telephones for a parent who is not home.

- Protect yourself by never letting a stranger know you are home alone.

- You may feel uncomfortable because you have to make up a story and pretend that a parent really is there. You have been taught to tell the truth, but when someone calls for an absent parent, you are rightly instructed to tell an untruth.

- When someone calls for your absent parent, ask the person to tell you her or his name. The person may sound like someone you know, but still, do not tell

the person your name or address even when you are
asked to do so. Do not give any information,
especially about when your parent will be home or
where your parent is.

• Some of the statements youngsters feel comfortable
saying are:

"My mom is resting and cannot be disturbed."

"My dad is busy and can't come to the phone. Can I
take a message and have him call you back?"

"My mom is in the shower and cannot come to the
phone right now."

"My dad is not feeling well and doesn't want to talk on
the phone."

"My dad is cleaning out the basement and cannot come
upstairs."

"My mom says to take a message. She'll call you back in
an hour" (or whenever you know she will be home).

• If a person is persistent, calmly hang up. Remember,
you are in charge of the phone.

TALKING IT OUT

Phone calls from friends or people a child knows are fun to
receive. Talking on the phone helps the child pass away the
time, allows children to share their feelings, and gives them
an opportunity to discuss homework or make plans for the
next day.

When a stranger calls and youngsters are alone, they become alarmed because their privacy has been intruded upon. They feel nervous knowing they have to make up a story, since they have been taught to always tell the truth to adults. The rules are now changed. Children worry about whether the person on the other end will believe them. Youngsters feel flustered if the caller is persistent.

To help youngsters better prepare themselves, mothers or fathers could role-play different situations that could arise. Children could act the part of the stranger and try out the many questions they think that person might ask. By asking the questions, children develop a sense of control over what could be an otherwise disquieting situation. When the parent takes on the role of caller, the children are able to decide what responses feel most comfortable for them to use in the future.

Since many youngsters will be by themselves when telephone calls come in for their mother or father, preparation is crucial. Parents must recognize that even if their children know what to say, they may still feel queasy when that unsuspecting call comes and they have to answer with a lie.

Disturbing Telephone Calls

Twelve-year-old Oliver has been getting weird telephone calls every day after school. At first, he thought it was probably someone from school who was disguising his voice and was just fooling around. But now that the calls have been coming several days in a row, he isn't sure. Maybe someone is watching him and will do something terrible. Now he is really scared.

How would you react if you were Oliver?

Have you ever received a scary telephone call? What did you do? What might you do now?

THINKING AHEAD

- An obscene or threatening phone call is terribly disturbing. You just don't feel safe.

- Since what a threatening phone caller wants most is a response from you, say nothing and hang up immediately. Engaging the caller in conversation only encourages him or her. Obscene and threatening calls will usually happen only once or twice if you don't respond to them.

- Some youngsters keep a whistle near the phone to blow into the receiver. The sharp sound surprises the caller and often ends these kind of calls.

- *Never let the caller know that you are home alone.*

- Although it's not easy, try to stay as calm as you can.

- After the first disturbing call, call your parent, a friend, or someone who will offer you comfort and advice. Have emergency phone numbers nearby. It is difficult to remember phone numbers when you are in a panic.

• Try to remember the conversation and write it down.

• After the telephone call, you might feel more comfortable and safer going to a friend's or neighbor's home. Wait there until your parent returns home.

• Harassing phone calls are illegal. If they continue, your parents should notify the telephone company to trace the voice.

• Keep a pad of paper next to the telephone. For each distyurbing call, write down the:

Time _____

Date _____

Length _____

Type of call (obscene, threatening, harassing)_____

What the person says_____

_____

Male or female_____

Age of person (try to estimate)_____

Tone of voice (high, low, muffled)_____

• Once the caller is identified, legal action can be taken.

- It can also be frightening when the phone rings and there is nobody on the other end. It could simply mean that the caller dialed the wrong number and hung up when you answered the phone. This happens to everyone.

- When the phone rings repeatedly and no one is on the other end, it is probably being done on purpose. Again, hang up.

- Sometimes parents may decide to change the telephone number and/or request an unlisted number.

TALKING IT OUT

A telephone call can bring help in times of emergency or companionship when one is lonely. Unfortunately, there are some people who abuse the telephone to bother others.

Most of the young people we interviewed are rightly fearful when a caller says something scary or obscene or calls repeatedly and then hangs up. They are alone and vulnerable, and they have good reason to feel upset.

All unwanted calls are startling, but not all of them are meant to be menacing. Sometimes friends fool around and dare one another to telephone. It maybe amusing to them, but it is not funny to the person on the receiving end. Each harassing call must be taken seriously, because some threats are real.

If an alarmed child calls a mother or father at work the parent should attempt to calm the child. Even after the phone conversation is over, the fears can linger. Children need to talk. They may repeat the scenario over and over again, not just at that moment but even for days or weeks afterward.

After the disturbing phone calls, youngsters may be afraid to be home alone. A thoughtful response by their parents enables them to better cope with this terrifying experience. Youngsters might be encouraged to bring a friend home with them or to go to someone else's house after school. An after-school sitter may be necessary for a while. Parents and children need to work out solutions to enable the children to feel more comfortable being by themselves. Obscene phone calls are verbal assaults that invade the minds of people of all ages.

Misplaced Keys

Ten-year-old Jonathan is in a great mood. It is report card day. He has been working hard in class, and he is excited that his grades have gone up. He got his first B in math! He runs home to call his mom and tell her the good news.

When he reaches in his pocket for his keys, they aren't there. Where could they be? Did he remember to take them to school? Could he have lost them? Jonathan's excitement now turns to panic.

What would you do if you came home from school and discovered that you didn't have your house keys?

Has this ever happened to you? If so, how did you feel?

THINKING AHEAD

- Before you leave for school each morning, make sure you have your keys with you. Check again before you leave school to go home. If there is an alarm system in your home, make sure the alarm key is on the key ring too.

- Keep your keys in a secure place, such as a zippered book bag. Make sure you keep your keys in the same place every day, and return them to that place after you use them so you know where they are at all times. Do not keep your keys in a place where they are visible or could fall out or be stolen.

- Duplicate keys can be left with a neighbor, friend, relative, or building superintendent in case you lose or misplace your own set.

- Decide with your parents who the possible key holders could be. Choose people who are close by and are generally home in the afternoon.

My key holders are:

Name _____

Address _____

Phone _____

Name _____

Address _____

Phone _____

- If the key holder is not at home, know where you may go until she or he returns.

- Wearing keys around your neck is a sign that you are going to an empty house. Don't do it—keep keys out of sight.

- There is no safety in leaving a key under a doormat, in a mailbox, or under a flowerpot. Many people can find hidden keys; there is no place that is secret from criminals.

- Do not write your name and address on your keys. Lost keys enable others to enter your house.

- If you suspect that your keys have been stolen, do not return to your house. Rather than risk an intruder, go to the home of a friend or neighbor. Call your parents. Do not return home until a security check has been made.

- If your keys are lost or stolen, your parents will want to change the locks to your home.

TALKING IT OUT

No matter how careful children try to be, there may be days that they forget, misplace, or lose their keys. This happens to everybody—even adults.

Most important, children should try not to panic. They may be especially upset if they hear the telephone ringing inside the house, feel hungry or hot, or have to go to the bathroom. They might sit down in front of their house or apartment to think about their available choices, including going to the key holder's house.

After they are safely back in their home, children should call their parents and explain what happened. Youngsters welcome a sympathetic voice to calm them down and let them know that even though they have misplaced their keys, what is most important to the parents is that they are okay.

Even though children may frequently be forgetful, it is their obligation to themselves and to their family to remember to take their keys every day. If youngsters consistently leave their keys at home or at school, this may be a sign that they are not yet ready for the responsibility of being on their own.

Chapter 4

Before and After School

Being by Yourself

Mornings are hectic in nine-year-old Lily's house. Everyone rushes around. Her dad leaves early to drop off her brother Jeremy at the day care center. Her mom has to be at work by 8:00 A.M. So Lily is home alone for forty-five minutes until she leaves for school.

Lily has a lot of responsibilities in the morning. She has to clean up the breakfast dishes and load them into the dishwasher. She must remember to take her lunch, bus pass, schoolbooks, and keys, and lock the door. Because she is afraid of missing the school bus, she is always at the bus stop ten minutes before it arrives.

What do you think goes on in Lily's mind in the morning?

What could Lily's parents do to make her mornings less hectic?

What are your mornings like?

How would you change them if you could?

THINKING AHEAD

- *Before your parents start leaving you home alone before school, talk about how you really feel about taking on such a responsibility.*

- If you are home alone in the morning, you should not have any other responsibilities beyond getting to school on time with your school belongings.

- Before they leave for work, your parents should see that you have eaten a well-balanced breakfast. (Elementary school teachers report that an increasing number of children are coming to school having had little or no breakfast or merely a doughnut or cookies. This leaves them ill prepared to begin the school day.)

- Proper clothing should be laid out so that you can be appropriately dressed. (Teachers and principals report that children home alone often come to school with no jacket or other protective attire.)

- Set a timer to remind you when to leave for school.

- Develop a checklist to help you remember what you need to bring each day.

Before School Checklist Daily Reminder

Day of the week:_____

Lunch

Books

Homework

Keys

Transportation pass

Money

Gym clothes/sneakers

School permission slips (when due)

Library books

EXTRAS

Musical instrument

Books for religious school

Clothing/equipment for after-school programs

TALKING IT OUT

Being left alone in the morning is disquieting for most elementary school children. They sit home marking time and watching television until it is time to leave for school. *Below the sixth-grade level, most children are neither ready nor willing to be without adult supervision in the morning.*

Principals told us that at least 25 percent of their students are already at the school door when they arrive for work. These children say that they would rather wait outside the school building for a half hour or more than be home alone.

Parents who presently have not yet found an alternative to leaving their youngsters unsupervised can still be supportive, loving, and appreciative of their children. They can spend a few extra minutes of undistracted time together before they leave for work. They can tell their youngsters that they understand how difficult it must be in having to get themselves to school. Parents should sympathize with their children's discomfort.

If parents leave for work before their children awaken, they could write a cheery note saying, "I love you," "Thinking of you," "Let's play basketball tonight," or "We are having dinner at Grandma's." Any note that communicates warm feelings is appreciated by children. If possible, parents should call from work and talk with their youngster before she or he departs for school. These shared morning conversations mean so much.

Parents should be alert for possible signs of stress in their children. Frequent physical complaints such as headaches or stomachaches in the morning could indicate that a child is not ready to be home alone before school and that supervision must be provided.

Public Transportation

Each day, eleven-year-old Alex boards the city bus with his friend Lamont to ride uptown to school. This morning Lamont is sick, and Alex is a uneasy about having to ride the bus alone, especially since a few days ago a group of kids boarded the bus and were bothering people. He just hopes they aren't there again this morning.

What precautions might Alex take?

Has anything frightening ever happened to you or anyone you know on the bus or subway?

THINKING AHEAD

- If you take public transportation, have your parents take you on a trial run. Count the number of stops to your destination, and locate the emergency alarm in case you ever need to alert the conductor. Determine the safest routes from your home to the public transportation stop and from the final stop to your school.

- Travel with friends—it's fun and safer.

- Keep your pass, money, or token in an accessible place. You might want to keep some extra change in a zippered pocket or other secure place.

- If you are late for the bus or subway, don't take a shortcut through alleys or wooded areas. *Never* accept a ride with someone you don't know well. Always have your parents' permission.

- If you forget or lose your money, borrow from a friend or teacher. If that is not possible, try to explain your circumstances to the driver and say you will repay the next day.

- If there are only a few passengers on the bus, sit near the driver. Choose a subway car with lots of people—usually a middle car.

- A person sitting next to you may act friendly to you and strike up a conversation. You should *not* answer the stranger's questions. Never give details about your name, where you live, or what school you attend.

• If someone sits next to you who makes you feel uncomfortable, move to another seat. If you are followed you, go to the conductor or another adult and say, "That person is bothering me." Don't be afraid to make a scene. Scream or yell to attract attention. Never leave the bus or subway alone if you think you are being followed.

TALKING IT OUT

Public transportation is an efficient way to go from one place to another. But children must learn to take precautions to be better prepared for the normal mishaps of a late bus or a misplaced transportation pass. Youngsters must also be aware of possible dangers, such as a person acting in an unruly or threatening manner. Being alert to their surroundings at all times enables children to respond appropriately.

If an unfortunate incident occurs, children may need to tell their parents about the event to work through their sense of fear. Parents should listen and respond sympathetically, then offer practical suggestions and ways to avoid future occurrences.

If a child is emotionally shaken, further action may be necessary. A parent may have to take a child to school, find alternative transportation, or arrange for the child to travel with classmates. When parents respond quickly and thoughtfully, children are better able to adjust to frightening situations.

Keeping Busy

Justin, a sixth grader, usually has a great time in the afternoon. Until last year, he attended the extended day program at his school. Now he comes home after school. He really likes being on his own, without anyone telling him what to do.

He feels free. He can invite a friend over, go to the library, ride his bike, or just be alone and listen to music. He loves his independence.

When you are bored, how do you entertain yourself?

What would you like the best and the least about being home alone in the afternoon?

THINKING AHEAD

- Keeping busy for a few hours after school is not easy. To keep from becoming bored or lonely, try to use your free time in a way that interests you.

- With your parents, plan next week's after-school schedule. Keep it posted as a reminder. At the end of this story are Weekly Activity Sheets for you to fill out to help you structure your week. Your weekly activity sheet could look something like this:

Monday   Visit the library. Check out books
                        and/or a video.

                        Straighten up room.

63

Tuesday	Invite a friend over.
	Play a game.
Wednesday	Religious school class.
	Listen to music.
Thursday	Go to a friend's/neighbor's house.
	Do homework.
Friday	Relax.
	Play at the community center.

• There are many ways to spend a busy, creative, enjoyable time after school. Among the activities you might choose are:

Reading. Your book choices are unlimited, from science fiction to romance to biography. Your school or local library can be a great resource. Your parents may also consider subscribing to magazines for you.

Hobbies. Start a new hobby, or spend more time with ones you already have. You might enjoy model building, weaving, astronomy, photography, crossword puzzles, or collecting baseball cards or stickers.

Music. Listen to tapes or the radio. Take dancing lessons. Learn to play a musical instrument.

Sports. Join a team at school or at the Y. Swim at the community center. Jog or walk with friends.

Art. Develop your creative side. Choose from painting,

drawing, pottery, calligraphy, graphics, and cartooning. Let your imagination take off.

Games. You can play games by yourself or with friends. Among the wide selection are cards, checkers, backgammon, chess, concentration, Scrabble, and the many commercial board games, as well as computer and video games.

Cooking. Have permission and know the rules before you use any electrical appliance or the stove. Fix yourself an exotic, healthy snack. Then clean up the exotic mess!

Homework. Though it's not as exciting as the above activities, completing part of your homework in the afternoon will give you more time to spend with your parents in the evening. Not everyone wants to spend time after school doing homework. Many children prefer to have their parents around when they do it. Choose what is best for you.

TALKING IT OUT

One of the major complaints of children home alone is boredom. A frequent remark from the youngsters we interviewed was, "I don't know what to do by myself all afternoon." Most youngsters look to their mothers and fathers for guidance since they do not possess the necessary ability to plan fulfilling afternoons for themselves day after day. Family meetings or individual discussions can help create alternatives to television watching.

Parents can explore the various afternoon programs at their child's school, library, or local community center.

There, youngsters can be with other children in a supervised setting for a part of the week with scheduled activities.

There is much for children to do at home—new skills to learn, ideas to pursue, and hobbies to develop. Children who are occupied in productive pursuits feel better about themselves. Mothers and fathers at work obviously want their youngsters at home to be happy. With careful planning, parents may even be able to curtail those afternoon phone calls that begin, "I have nothing to do."

WEEKLY ACTIVITY SHEET

This week I would like to:

Monday   _____

  _____

Tuesday   _____

  _____

Wednesday   _____

  _____

Thursday   _____

  _____

Friday   _____

Television

The first thing that eleven-year-old Rhodie does when she comes home from school is turn on the television set. She loves to watch one soap after another. She pauses only long enough to go into the kitchen for some food.

At 5:00 P.M. Rhodie rushes over and turns off her programs before her mother comes home from work. She knows her mom doesn't like her watching too much television, especially some of those afternoon shows.

Why do you think you like to turn on the television when you come home from school?

Are you ever frightened by some of the shows you watch?

THINKING AHEAD

- Television helps you fill up the hours you spend by yourself. The noise can make you feel as if someone is with you. But it's important that watching television not be the most fulfilling activity for you every day.

- Did you know that young people spend more time watching television than eating, reading, and playing combined?

- Write down the amount of time you actually spend each day in front of the television. Work out with your parents the amount of time that you all feel is appropriate. Be selective. Some programs can be

67

scary and disturbing when you watch them alone.

• Your mom or dad might occasionally rent a video movie or borrow one from the library to insure that what you are watching is appealing to you.

• With your parents, look at the television schedule for next week and decide on the number of hours and the types of programs you will watch. Use the Weekly Television Calendar.

WEEKLY TELEVISION CALENDAR

Monday
Program(s) _____

Time(s) _____

Tuesday
Program(s) _____

Time(s) _____

Wednesday
Program(s) _____

Time(s) _____

Thursday
Program(s) _____

Time(s) _____

Friday
Program(s) _____

Time(s) _____

TALKING IT OUT

By the time most children finish high school, they have logged 20,500 hours in front of the television screen and only 16,500 hours in school. Many youngsters report that they are bored or lonely and that watching television gives them something to do in the afternoons. Television becomes the passive companion.

An average of 5.7 acts of violence are shown every hour that youngsters are glued to the set. These shows can intensify children's fears and create emotional stress.

When children spend too much time viewing television, they do not utilize their energies in creative endeavors. Neither their minds nor bodies are being exercised. Parents help children when they limit their television viewing and plan afternoons rich in diverse activities with their youngsters.

Friends

A couple of days a week, twelve-year-old Rebecca invites friends over after school. They play tennis together, do homework, talk about school, and generally have a good time.

Today is different.

During the last period of the day, Lorin asks Rebecca if she—Lorin—can go to Rebecca's apartment with her. Even though Rebecca doesn't know Lorin very well, Rebecca says, "Sure." After they arrive at Rebecca's apartment, the girls make themselves a snack, but Lorin does not clean up her mess. She starts to call kids and hang up on them when they answer the phone. Rebecca tells Lorin to stop. Lorin gets angry. Rebecca wants Lorin to leave, but she is afraid to tell her.

What do you think Rebecca should do?

Have any of your friends made you feel uncomfortable or acted in a way that upset you when you were alone together? If so, what did you do?

THINKING AHEAD

• Check with your parents before you invite someone to your home.

• With your parents, establish guidelines for acceptable conduct. When your friends come over, for example:

No one is allowed in a parent's room.

No eating in any room but the kitchen.

No food or dishes left around.

No ball playing indoors.

No misuse of the telephone.

No jackets on floor.

No using a sibling's belongings without permission.

No fighting.

You might want to have these rules posted in a prominent place so your friends will understand what is expected of them as well. You might say, "My parents are pretty strict about what happens when they're not here."

- Invite only friends you trust and know are responsible. Good friends are people who care about you.

- If a person has never been to your house before, do not invite him or her when no parents are at home.

- Be choosy whom you select. Someone who acts up in school may act up in your house too.

- Never invite someone of the opposite sex over without a parent's approval and without someone older and responsible present.

- Be cautious about inviting someone over who wants to be with you because your parents aren't home.

- If your friends act up, ask them to leave.

- Do not "show off" by breaking accepted family rules.

- Know whom you can call if things get out of hand.

TALKING IT OUT

Children, like adults, enjoy the company of their peers. Parents recognize that it is important to children to be able to bring friends home after school, and they often encourage their youngsters to be with someone.

Time passes more quickly when a child shares the afternoon with another person. Friends ease their loneliness. Having another person around is comforting—noises don't seem so loud, and the darkness less alarming.

By allowing children to invite over a friend, parents demonstrate that they trust their youngsters. In turn, children must be willing to accept this trust and not abuse it.

Having friends over is a responsibility. Children should not let others take advantage of them. It usually does not work out well when more than two people visit at one time.

If the house gets messed up or something is broken, children need to understand that even if it wasn't their fault, their parents may become angry and place new restrictions on who can visit. Parents should be as understanding as possible when such incidents occur. Children are already frightened, and they may feel guilty as well. Mothers and fathers should first listen to the child's explanation and not immediately place blame. After all, items break when parents are home too. If the child demonstrates responsible behavior in the future, parents usually allow the incident to become history.

Leaving the House

It is 4:30 in the afternoon, and Lisa is getting bored. Her sister isn't due home from track practice for an hour and a half, and her dad won't be home from work until 6:30. She has already finished her English homework and practiced the piano. She takes out an ice cream sandwich to eat. Happily, the phone rings. Her friend Stacey is calling to ask her to come over with a bathing suit to go swimming in Stacey's pool.

Lisa quickly changes her clothes, grabs a towel, and races down the block to Stacey's. Before leaving, she writes a note telling her dad where she is.

What do you think of Lisa's actions?

What are you supposed to do when you leave the house and your parents are still at work?

THINKING AHEAD

- Before you make plans to leave the house, be sure your mom or dad approves.

- Decide with your parents which friends' houses you can visit. Questions to consider: Do they live nearby? Can you get there safely and easily? Will there be supervision?

- If you can't contact a parent at work, leave a message with a co-worker stating where you will be,

the phone number where you may be reached,
and your expected time of arrival back home.

- *Be home before dark,* especially if you are going to
  be somewhere other than at a friend's.

- If you are delayed coming home, call your parent
  immediately. If you cannot reach your mother or
  father, contact a neighbor, friend, or relative and ask
  them to keep calling your parent to explain your
  lateness.

- Know at least two people to call, other than your
  parents, if you need a ride home.

- When using public transportation, be aware of bus
  or train schedules and carry these with you.

- Carry extra money, including change for a pay
  phone.

TALKING IT OUT

Most children told us that they prefer to spend time with a
friend in the afternoon rather than be by themselves. When
possible, plans should be made in advance, with parents'
approval. But youngsters, like adults, also make arrangements on the spur of the moment. During school, a child
may ask a friend to come over the house, go to the library, or
even to the dentist's. Or once at home, the youngster may
receive an invitation to visit a friend.

To insure that youngsters can make responsible choices,
parents and children should discuss guidelines for going out
after school. Youngsters need to understand that parents

have certain expectations of them: they should keep parents informed of their whereabouts, observe personal safety rules, and be home at the agreed-upon time.

When youngsters respond maturely to new freedoms extended to them, their mothers and fathers know that they are able to handle this new experience. Praising youngsters for exhibiting good judgment and trustworthiness encourages further responsible actions. If, on the other hand, children do not return home on time, or if they seem uncomfortable discussing what they did or where they went, they are not ready for the privilege of visiting others after school. In time, these youngsters may be better able to handle this responsibility with careful parental monitoring.

Youngsters need to be able to join friends in the afternoon or to go out by themselves. But parents also need to know where their children are, whom they are with, and that they are safe so that they will have peace of mind.

Walking around the Neighborhood

Twelve-year-old Meghan takes a public bus to and from school every day. The bus stop is a block from her apartment, and there are lots of people in the mornings waiting with her. But when she returns home at 2:30 P.M., there are few people around.

Lately, a group of older boys has been hanging around the store where Meghan stops to get a snack on her way home. Usually they ignore Meghan, but today one of them whistles and calls out to her.

Now Meghan is upset. She doesn't want to change her routine, but she also doesn't want to be bothered by these boys.

What do you think Meghan should do?

How safe do you feel walking around your neighborhood?

Are there places you avoid going near?

Has someone in your neighborhood ever frightened you? If so, what did you do? Did you discuss this experience with your mother or father?

THINKING AHEAD

- *Be a detective.* Walk around your neighborhood with your mom or dad. Be on the lookout for unsafe places, such as a dangerous intersection, a wooded or isolated area, a building under construction, or a house with an unfriendly dog.

  What places frighten you?

  1. _____

  2. _____

  3. _____

  4. _____

- In your walk around your neighborhood, decide with your parents which are the safer areas. They may be places where there is adult supervision such as your school, a recreation center, or an afternoon program at your church or synagogue.

- Decide with your parents two homes you can go to in the afternoon in case of an emergency. An emergency is anything that frightens, disturbs, or upsets you. Write down the names, addresses, and phone numbers of these emergency homes.

- Be alert to possible danger signs, such as an unfamiliar car parked near your house or a "creepy" person hanging around your apartment lobby.

- Some communities have designated certain people's houses as Safe Homes, Block Parents, or Neighborhood Watch Places, where children may go if they are afraid. Find out if your neighborhood has such a place, and if so, write down the location of the house.

- Decide with your parents which stores or other places you could go to if you need help fast.

- Your parents may suggest that your teacher or school principal invite a law enforcement officer to class to discuss how to make a neighborhood safer and children feel secure.

TALKING IT OUT

Some communities are obviously safer than others. Some neighborhoods are isolated, while others bustle with activity. Some apartment buildings employ attendants to provide additional security, while in other dwellings children may be afraid to enter their elevator or walk out in the hall for fear of whom they might meet.

When youngsters know and trust their neighbors, they feel more secure in their environment. Mothers and fathers can help youngsters by introducing them to neighbors so they are no longer strangers to be avoided or feared. Children who know only a few people in their community have fewer resources in case of an emergency.

Children should make a commitment to their parents that they will venture only to those areas agreed to be safer. Whenever they leave the house, they must keep their parents informed of their whereabouts. Youngsters need to stay alert to people who make them feel uneasy and afraid, and they should be prepared to respond quickly and knowingly.

With the cooperation of parents, schools, police departments, local governments, and civic groups, a growing number of communities are establishing securer neighborhoods. These plans should be supported by everyone who cares about youngsters' physical safety and emotional well-being.

Chores

Eleven-year-old Vanessa feels that her mom asks too much of her. When she comes home from school, she is expected to make the beds, set the table, and tidy up. She doesn't mind helping out—after all, her mom is working hard too. But Vanessa thinks her brother Kevin should also have to do some chores. She needs more time to be with her friends or just do nothing.

What are your after-school responsibilities?

How are these chores assigned?

THINKING AHEAD

- Most children are expected to perform some chores around the house.

- Assignments might be divided so that some days you may have responsibilities but other days you are free.

- Family meetings are a meaningful way to discuss ideas and complaints and decide on the next week's responsibilities.

- Chores should not be assigned by whether you are a girl or a boy.

- It helps if your parents are clear in detailing what they expect you to do.

- Post your duties on a bulletin board, and check off each task as you complete it.

TALKING IT OUT

Some children who come home from school perform few if any chores; others are assigned a significant part of the housework. It depends on the needs of the family, the expectations of parents, and the willingness of youngsters.

Many children feel good about sharing family responsibilities. Their chores keep them busy and make the time pass faster. Then, when their mothers or fathers return from work, they have more time together.

In our survey, more than half the children reported that they have additional chores because their parents work. A large number of these children are overwhelmed by their extra household responsibilities. Even children who are mature and responsible need after-school time just to be children. When youngsters are burdened with too many tasks at too young an age, they frequently feel stressed-out even before they reach adolescence.

The chores children do need to be realistic and geared to their capabilities. Teaching youngsters to assume responsibilities is a continuous process. Children are more accepting of performing chores when their assignments are clearly explained, they have input into decisions, and know the chore's importance to the family structure.

Mothers and fathers are role models. Of the youngsters we surveyed, 78 percent stated that their mothers did most of the work in the house, while only twelve percent mentioned their fathers as willing participants in housework. When both parents are actively involved in running the household, boys as well as girls are more receptive to doing their chores.

Of course, there will be times when children will not perform their tasks the way their parents expect. Parents should attempt to maintain a degree of flexibility as well as a sense of humor. Youngsters do not work with the consistency, skill, and efficiency of adults.

Children perform their chores more willingly when they are complimented. Praise gives youngsters a deeper appreciation of their value and skills, as well as enhances their self-esteem.

Babysitting

Twelve-year-old Sam has to take care of his little sister, Marnie, after school. He doesn't mind watching her once in a while, but he feels that three days a week is asking too much. He says it's not fair that he has so much responsibility. He worries, too, that something might happen to his sister when they are together. He feels pretty frustrated.

What should Sam do?

What could Sam's parents do?

If you babysit for a sibling, how would you describe this situation?

THINKING AHEAD

- Some parents do rely on older children to care for their younger siblings. This should be an occasional alternative to regular, adult-supervised child care arrangements.

- Try to be flexible and willing to fill in when your parents need you to babysit.

- Together, families need to sit down and establish specific rules about babysitting.

Friends of the babysitter-sibling who are allowed over

Friends of the babysat-sibling who are allowed over

Acceptable snacks

Permissible television programs

Telephone limits

Chores to be completed

Inside/outside areas for play

Time parent is expected home

Special instructions for the day

- Know what to do in case of an emergency.

- Try to concentrate on taking care of your sibling. It's an important job.

- *Never* use physical force or verbal abuse when your sibling acts up. Report the misbehavior to your parents. If a sibling is creating a situation that you can't handle, know the phone number of a relative or neighbor whom you can call to come over and help you out.

- Regular family meetings can help resolve differences.

TALKING IT OUT

Occasionally acting as a babysitter after school affords a fifth, sixth, or seventh grader the opportunity to learn how to take care of their younger brothers or sisters. Many of these youngsters are flattered by their parents' trust in them and enjoy the companionship of their sibling. They may even be pleased to make an important contribution to their family.

But parental expectations must be realistic. Older children need time free from babysitting responsibilities to participate in sports and clubs, be with friends, and be alone. Certainly there are occasions when they can be asked to take care of a younger sister or brother, but not on a consistent, everyday basis. Parents should recognize that younger siblings, too, may resent being told what to do by a brother or sister who is only a few years older. In turn, the older child may complain that no one listens. These common problems must be addressed to ensure family harmony.

Complimenting youngsters for their helpful behavior is always appreciated. Giving an occasional present or extra privileges is a good acknowledgment of gratitude.

Chapter 5

Emergencies—Minor and Major

Stomachache

Aaron is home alone after school doing his home-work. Suddenly, he has a cramp in his stomach that really hurts. He wonders whether it's something he ate for lunch. He goes to the bathroom, but he still doesn't feel better. A half hour later, he still feels awful.

What do you think Aaron should do?

What would you do if you had a stomachache?

THINKING AHEAD

- Call your parent.

- Think about reasons why your stomach is upset. Did you overeat? Could you be reacting to something you are allergic to? Have you recently been exposed to the flu? Your stomach could be affected by emotional distress, such as getting a bad grade on a test or having an argument with a friend. There could be a more serious cause, such as appendicitis, but this is much less common.

- Take your temperature. Do you have a fever?

- Do you have any nausea? Do you feel like vomiting? Do you have diarrhea?

- Lie down quietly. This may help the pain go away.

- *Never take any medicines without your parent's approval.*

- Do not take any food or drink. If you are thirsty, have only a few sips of water.

TALKING IT OUT

Everyone has stomachaches, but usually the pain goes away quickly and people soon feel better. Still, abdominal pain is scary, and children should not hesitate to call a parent, friend, neighbor, or relative if it arises. Youngsters need comforting and a telephone "hug."

It is essential for parents to understand the cause of this discomfort. Is the child afraid of being home after school? Are there pressures at school? Abdominal pain can be an indicator of emotional distress, especially when it recurs in a pattern. If stomachaches persist, parents may need to seek professional help.

Cut

Nine-year-old Jennifer is making herself a peanut butter sandwich. While she cuts the bread, the plate slips and crashes to the floor. As she picks up the broken pieces, she cuts her hand, and it begins to bleed. Her hand starts to throb, and she begins to cry.

What do you think Jennifer should do?

Have you ever cut yourself? If so, what did you do?

THINKING AHEAD

- Before you touch an open wound, scrub your hands. Wash and rinse the cut area with soap and warm water.

- Hold a clean cloth or paper towel against the cut, and press for a few minutes until the bleeding stops. Put on a sterile pad or bandage to protect the area.

- You may apply first-aid cream that is used for cuts, but don't use any medicines without your parents' permission.

- Do not put your mouth on a cut. Your mouth harbors germs that could infect the wound.

- If a sliver of glass is in the wound, call an adult. Medical attention is needed to assure that all particles have been removed.

- If swelling occurs, apply a clean washcloth with ice in a plastic bag or a cold compress.

- Call for help immediately if the bleeding continues, is severe, or you feel faint.

TALKING IT OUT

All youngsters cut themselves, but this experience is especially scary for a child home alone. Regardless of the severity of the cut, many children wish to call their mothers or fathers for some tender loving care. Parents should know in advance how to act quickly and effectively help their youngsters take charge of this emergency.

Burn

It is cold and rainy as Julia walks home from elementary school. All she is thinking about is making herself some hot noodle soup. When she gets home, she empties the can into a pan and turns on the stove. In a couple of minutes her soup is ready. She quickly pours the boiling liquid into a bowl, but some of it splashes on her hand. Her hand begins to turn red, and she screams in pain.

What do you think Julia should do now?

Have you ever burned yourself? What did you do?

THINKING AHEAD

- Minor burns can be very painful for everybody.

- Since a burn feels hot, soak the sore part in cool water for at least ten minutes.

- Never put ice on the burn because of the possibility of further damage.

- Loosely cover the burn with a clean bandage.

- Don't put first aid cream on the wound.

- If blisters form, leave them alone. Don't try to open them because you will increase the chance of infection.

- *If the burn is severe, call for help immediately.* Call a parent, friend, neighbor, pediatrician, police, emergency medical technicians, or anyone you trust who can respond quickly. Until help arrives, keep the injured area under cool water. Try to remain as calm as you can, even though this is easier said than done.

TALKING IT OUT

The most common household injury is first-degree burns. All people are careless at times, because they are focusing more on a television program, a phone conversation, or a song on the radio than on what they are cooking on the stove.

Burns are painful, and it's natural to be frightened. Mothers and fathers should calmly discuss what caused the accident and help their youngster learn from this incident so it does not soon happen again.

Injury

Every Tuesday after school, ten-year-old Ella has her friends Latisha and Jessica come over to keep one another company. These afternoons are special to them.

Today they are going to work on their science

project together, collecting different types of leaves and grasses. The girls take their notebooks and start to walk around the block. Suddenly, as Ella reaches down to pick up a few blades of grass, she is stung by a bee. She screams, and the girls all run back to Ella's house.

What do you think Ella and her friends should do?

Does your house have a first-aid kit? Have you been instructed in its safe use?

THINKING AHEAD

- Since you are home alone, you need a first-aid kit for minor medical problems. Understand its proper use.

- First-aid kits should be kept in a cool, dry place. Included in the kit should be a telephone list, with numbers of your parents, neighbors, physician, pharmacy, and poison control center.

- Read the label every time you use an item, since many boxes and bottles look alike.

- Parents should check the expiration date of all items.

A basic first-aid kit should include:

Item	Purpose
Thermometer	Take temperature and check for fever

Box of bandages in various sizes	Cover small cuts
Sterile gauze pads	Dress large wounds
Adhesive tape	Hold bandages in place
Small scissors	Cut adhesive tape
Cotton swabs	Clean cuts
Tweezers	Remove splinters and stingers
Baking soda or calomine lotion	Treat insect bites and poison ivy
Cold pack	Prevent or limit swelling
Aspirin substitute	Help pain of headache and reduce fever
Ipecac syrup	Induce vomiting in case of poisoning. *Always call a parent, physician, or poison control center first.*

TALKING IT OUT

Safety experts agree that every home should have a special first-aid kit for children. Some of them call it a "first and last aid" kit, since most youngsters can handle small injuries without having to call a parent. Local Red Cross chapters and some schools provide first-aid training.

If youngsters have any doubts as to how to proceed, they must first call their mother, father, pediatrician, or health clinic. Parents should praise their youngster's ability to handle these situations. Parents' own medications should be locked away so that youngsters cannot use them either accidentally or experimentally.

Telephoning for Help

Twelve-year-old Dimitri said that this was the worst day of his life. It is the first baseball game of the season, and he is the starting second baseman. He dashes home from school to change into his uniform. Running down the stairs, he trips and falls and hears something snap. He can't move his arm, and he starts to scream.

What should Dimitri do?

Have you ever had an emergency? If so, how did you handle the situation?

THINKING AHEAD

- Major injuries include:

  severe bleeding

  lightheadedness, dizziness, feeling of losing consciousness

  experiencing a great deal of pain

  possible broken bones

poisoning

bad burn or scalding

difficulty in breathing, speaking, or swallowing

injury to an eye or ear

being bitten by an animal or insect

Immediate aid and professional help are required

- If you are not quite sure how serious the problem is, you still need to be cautious. Delaying treatment can further aggravate the problem.

- Call your parents, police, physician, ambulance, hospital, or poison control center. Emergency numbers should be posted near the telephones in your house. Safety authorities suggest phones with special buttons for hospital, police, parents, and pediatrician. If you are unable to dial the number, dial 0 for operator, or in some places 911. Let the person know that this is an emergency!

- When you call, try to speak slowly and clearly so that the person can hear you correctly. Identify yourself:

My name is ⎯⎯⎯⎯⎯⎯⎯⎯⎯⎯⎯⎯

Describe briefly the problem ⎯⎯⎯⎯⎯⎯⎯

Telephone number you are calling from ⎯⎯⎯⎯

You are now at _____

        Street

    _____

        Apartment

    _____

        Town or City

Parent's names _____

Business phone number _____

Don't hang up until the other party has told you how to proceed and has assured you that help is on the way.

- Try not to move. Lie down, keep yourself warm, and stay as calm as you can.

- You need your parents' support. If you can't contact them yourself, ask the person who is assisting you to call them.

TALKING IT OUT

Accidents are the leading cause of death among children. Every year in the United States, approximately fourteen thousand youngsters lose their lives, and an additional twenty-three million are seriously hurt. Children home alone are especially vulnerable. More than half the children we interviewed who were thirteen years or younger did not know how to act appropriately in time of crisis.

Since emergencies happen quickly, time is of the essence.

Children home alone must be instructed on how to respond to these particularly difficult circumstances.

Avoiding Accidents

Eleven-year-old Alison is home alone waiting for her friend Karen to come over. When the bell rings, Alison rushes to open the door. She slips on the scatter rug and falls on the floor. She is bruised and upset. She's glad she didn't break anything. Slowly, she pulls herself up and lets Karen in.

Have you ever had an accident at home that could have been avoided?

How could your house be made safer?

THINKING AHEAD

- Creating a safer home while you are there alone takes careful thought and planning. Of course, every home is different, but there are some commonsense approaches to accident prevention that you and your mother and father should take.

- Before they leave you alone, your parents should make sure that:

Slip-proof mats are placed under all scatter rugs.

Closets are carefully arranged so that the items stored won't fall down when the door is opened.

Bookcases are firmly anchored.

Safety plugs are placed in unused electrical outlets.

Loose wires or frayed cords are repaired.

Poisonous cleaning supplies and other dangerous substances are locked in a secure place.

Household tools and supplies are stored away properly.

Wells are securely covered.

Pool areas are fenced in and locked.

TALKING IT OUT

Every year in the United States, about fourteen thousand children lose their lives in accidents of various kinds. Accidents are the leading cause of death in childhood, surpassing all children's diseases. Many other children are injured and handicapped for the rest of their lives. More than one-third of these accidents occur in the children's home.

Severe injury from an accident takes but a moment to happen. The time for prevention is before the mishap occurs. Every child and parent should have a home safety review from time to time. Look for objects or situations that could present possible hazards.

Chapter 6

Alarming Situations

Being Followed by a Stranger

One afternoon, eleven-year-old Judi is walking home from school, and she feels that someone is following her. She looks around and sees a man walking close behind her. He looks familiar, but Judi still feels uncomfortable. She starts to walk quickly, then breaks into a run. She is not sure if she should go to her house, since no one is there. She remembers that her friend Melissa had someone follow her a couple of weeks ago.

What do you think Judi should do?

Have you ever felt that someone was following you? If so, what did you do?

THINKING AHEAD

- Strangers are people you don't know. They may be men or women, boys or girls. Many of them are good, kind individuals who are just walking in the same direction as you are. But some people can be dangerous. That is why for safety's sake, be careful and always pay attention to what is happening around you.

- If you have any questions about whether a person is

following you, don't take chances. It's better to be cautious than to be sorry.

- Don't go near the stranger—maintain a good distance.

- Avoid making eye contact with the stranger. Try to look busy so that the person will feel less free to speak with or bother you.

- Do not answer any stranger who stops and asks, "How can I get to _____?"

- If someone pulls up in a car and calls to you, ignore him or her. Keep walking. Cross the street. Reverse your direction. Run away and scream for help if the stranger stops the car.

- Tell someone right away if you think you are being followed. Most adults will want to help, but you must ask them. Police officers obviously are the best people to contact, but when you need assistance quickly, choose the person closest to you.

- Be aware of safe places in your neighborhood in case of an emergency.

- Never get into an elevator if there is someone inside that makes you nervous.

- *Do not go into your apartment or house alone* if you think you are being followed. You would only show the person where you live. Find a neighbor or friend's house or a store, and immediately call your mother or father.

- Afterward, try to recall what the stranger looked like—height, hair color, approximate age, wearing glasses, sound of voice, clothing—as well as what the car looked like (color, make, any license plate numbers or letters), so you can provide the police with the information.

TALKING IT OUT

It can be upsetting for children to see a stranger close behind them, even if the person is harmless. Parents understand that they must teach their children precautions, even while they encourage them to explore the world around them. Sensible preparation gives young people a greater sense of confidence and heightened sense of awareness.

Mothers and fathers should encourage their children to stay with friends whenever possible. There is safety in numbers, since molesters generally do not accost groups of youngsters.

If someone approaches a child in an endangering way, the child will certainly need a great deal of parental support and love. Their ideal of the world has been shattered. Putting back the pieces will be difficult for them. The youngster should have an opportunity to recount the disturbing incident and express his or her anxiety and fear. For a period of time, the child may need to stay with someone to feel protected. Parents will have to make alternative plans to accommodate this. Slowly a youngster should be able to venture out alone again. If the child appears particularly apprehensive or exhibits other signs of stress, his or her parents could consider having the youngster speak with a professional counselor.

Parents should consider building a neighborhood support system and working with others to create a more child-safe community.

Fire

When twelve-year-old Emily comes home from field hockey practice after school, she is famished. She pulls out a pizza from the freezer, pops it into the microwave, then puts a movie into the VCR.

Emily is so absorbed in what she is watching that she forgets about her food. Suddenly she smells smoke and begins to panic.

What do you think Emily should do next?

Have you ever been alone when a fire broke out? How did you handle the situation?

THINKING AHEAD

- Never use the stove, toaster, microwave, or any other appliance until your parent explains it to you and demonstrates its safe usage. Make sure you understand all directions and precautions.

- Your parents should keep a fire extinguisher in the house, with clear instructions on how to use it. A smoke detector should be placed on each floor, especially near the kitchen and bedrooms. Your parents should test each detector each month by holding a small candle or lighter six inches from the sensor.

- Fires often start because of people's carelessness. Your parents should keep matches out of the reach of children.

- A valuable safety precaution is to know what to do if a fire does break out. Learn how to smother a small fire on the stove or toaster oven. If you cannot put the fire out easily and quickly, or if the flames are shooting up and seem out of control, leave your house or apartment as soon as possible. Shout as loudly as you can to alert other people.

- Know what to do if you catch on fire. When you are out of the burning house, *stop, drop, lie down, and roll back and forth*. If possible, wrap yourself in a blanket or coat to smother the flames. If outside, roll in the dirt, sand, or snow. Remove your burning clothes if you can, but never pull them over your head. Get medical help as soon as you can.

- If a room is smoking, crawl on your hands and knees to the exit.

- Know an escape route. Have your parents devise a step-by-step plan in case of an emergency. Plan two possible routes.

- As you leave the burning house or apartment, don't lock the door behind you. Firefighters need to be able to enter quickly.

- A house with two stories should have a commercial escape ladder, in case the stairway is blocked by flames.

- If you live in an apartment, use the nearest safe stairs. *Never* take the elevator in a burning building.

- Once you are out of danger, go to the nearest neighbor and call the fire department. State your name and address clearly. Do not hang up until you are sure that the person at the other end has understood the exact location of your house or apartment building.

- When possible, sound the fire alarm in the apartment or outside in the street.

- Call your mother or father. If someone on the other end says that your parent is busy, say it is an emergency and that you must speak to her or him immediately.

- *Never,* ever return to the burning house or apartment building under any conditions.

- Space heaters are a special fire hazard. You should not use them when no adult is home.

- Be prepared. Take in a fire prevention class. Many local fire departments, schools, and the Red Cross give instruction for small groups of young people. Many fire departments offer home safety checks when they are requested.

TALKING IT OUT

Experts estimate that one-third of all fire victims are children. In some cities, one in six calls responded to by the fire department involve youngsters home alone.

It is scary for children by themselves to smell smoke or see something burning. Their natural reaction may be to become numb and forget everything they have learned about how to handle it. When people feel their safety is threatened, it is very difficult for them to think clearly. But it is precisely these circumstances that require the most thoughtful preparation. Children should be taught that the *heroic act* is to leave a fire that cannot easily and quickly be contained. They should understand that they are not responsible for saving the house or any "valuables." Mothers and fathers need to emphasize that their only concern is their children's lives. Nothing else matters.

Youngsters who use cooking appliances have a responsibility to themselves and to their parents to do so cautiously. If a fire does break out, mothers and fathers need to find out the cause of the blaze. They need to speak in a concerned manner and not immediately place blame. Parents must determine whether their youngster was reckless or showed poor judgment. If so, their youngster clearly is not yet ready for the responsibility of being unsupervised.

Burglary

Twelve-year-old Ned is in a great mood as he walks home from school. His science exam was easier

TeachingYour Child to Be Home Alone

than he expected. His friend Christopher has invited him to spend the weekend at his uncle's farm, and today is Thursday.

Ned's mood quickly changes when he arrives at his house. As he puts his key in the front door, he notices that the living-room window is open. He is positive that it was closed when he left that morning for school. "Suppose there is a robber inside," he thinks, "and I'm all by myself!" Ned begins to shake.

What should Ned do?

What would you do if you came home and thought your home had been burglarized?

THINKING AHEAD

- *Never* enter your home if you notice an open door or window or hear a strange noise.

- Leave the area immediately. Go for help to a neighbor's or friend's house or building superintendent.

- Call the police and your parents.

- Do not return until the premises have been thoroughly examined by a responsible adult.

- If you find an intruder, try to stay as calm as possible. You might pretend that you are in the wrong apartment or house and leave as quickly as possible. Try to remember everything you can about the intruder—approximate height, weight, clothing, distinguishing features—and if you are able, note the type, color and license plate of the vehicle he was driving.

- Your personal safety is all that matters. Don't try to be a hero.

TALKING IT OUT

Burglaries occur in all neighborhoods. Fears of intruders are real. Children home alone need to be prepared for this emergency.

Therefore, preventive measures must be taken: doors locked, windows securely latched, ladders removed, peepholes installed, shrubbery cut, and elevators and hallways brightly lit. Children tell us that they feel safer when their house or apartment is equipped with an alarm system.

Parents must not give a gun to youngsters to protect themselves because they usually become the chief victims. Forty percent of all firearm fatalities involve children under nineteen years of age. Every day, one child fifteen years old or under dies in a handgun accident. The element of surprise is in the intruder's favor. A child could also mistakenly shoot a parent, sibling, or friend who came home early.

Children who have encountered an intruder or walked into a burglarized home will benefit from a lot of emotional support. They probably will not feel secure in their own home and will require company after school.

Children should be encouraged to talk about their emotional shock. They need comfort: "It must have been so frightening." They need reassurance: "We are going to do everything possible so this will not happen again." Youngsters' anxiety may be expressed not only in words but in sleeplessness, stomachaches, headaches, fatigue, irritability, or depression. If necessary, parents should seek professional counseling to help their youngster better cope with this trauma.

Being Aware of Good and Bad Touching

Alice, a sixth grader, hates it when her uncle comes over to her house in the afternoon. He knows she is by herself. He always wants to kiss and hug her. Once he tried to touch private parts of her body. He keeps saying, "Don't you know how much I love you?"

Alice is confused. She wonders if she should tell her parents. She is afraid they will think she is just being silly or exaggerating. But Alice is really afraid to be alone with her uncle.

What should Alice do?

What do you think Alice's parents should do?

What would you do if someone touched you in an inappropriate way?

THINKING AHEAD

- Most people who hug and kiss you do so because it is a wonderful way to show affection.

- Discuss with your parents the difference between *"good"* and *"bad"* touching.

- You do *not* have to accept kisses, hugs, or touching from anyone. State clearly that you will not tolerate this behavior. No adult or youth has the right to insist on any physical contact with you.

- If someone touches you in any way that makes you feel uncomfortable (even if that person is someone you know and might threaten to hurt you), immediately notify your parent or someone you can trust. Remember, no matter what anybody says, a child is the innocent victim.

- Seventy-eight percent of sexual abusers are not strangers but people the youngster knows well—a member of the family, a neighbor, a friend of the victim's family, or a friend.

Talking It Out

Sexual abuse is a real threat—for good reason. A 1992 Federally funded study states that almost sixty-two percent of women were raped when they were still minors. Twenty-nine percent of these girls were younger than age eleven when raped. For males, the number is ten percent. There has been a two hundred percent increase in the reporting of sexual abuse of young people in the last ten years, and this same study found that only sixteen percent of rape victims reported the assault to the police. Understandably, young people by themselves are especially easy targets.

Parents must not wait until an unfortunate incident takes place in their community before they address this vital concern with their youngsters. If children are old enough to become victims, they are old enough to receive reliable information about sexuality and sexual abuse.

Youngsters should be able to communicate their fears and feelings with their mothers and fathers. Children who are abused cannot understand why any adult would behave this way. They may not want to believe that this is actually happening to them. They may feel ashamed for being touched. But they must be made to understand that they are not responsible. It is not their fault.

Since some youngsters may not feel comfortable telling a parent what has occurred, adults should be aware of the following nonverbal clues:

- Fear of staying alone with a particular person

- Mood changes when that individual's name is mentioned or the person is invited over

- Symptoms of inner distress, such as headaches, stomachaches, sleeplessness, lack of concentration

- Genital trauma, soreness, or infection

Children who have been abused must be reassured that they will never again be alone with the molester. A professional counselor specifically trained in child abuse should be consulted. Going for help is a sign of strength and courage, enabling the family to begin a healing process after a traumatic experience.

For children and parents, this may be the hardest section of the book to read. It's difficult for most families to discuss child molestation. Hopefully, your family will never have to face this terrible ordeal. But children home alone must be prepared for every emergency.

Chapter 7

Testing
Yourself

Readiness Scale

You are obviously a parent who cares. That is why you are reading a book to prepare your child to be home alone.

We have devised a Readiness Scale to assist you in determining whether your youngster is capable of being in an unsupervised setting. You will be able to assess both what your child knows and what needs further discussion.

Have your child read each statement carefully and circle his or her response. Then total the score. At the conclusion, you will find a useful chart to enable you to decide if and when your youngster is able to take on this challenging responsibility.

0 = Child has no background or knowledge of what to do

1 = Child has a vague understanding of what to do

2 = Child is generally aware of what to do

I Know . . .

0 1 2   1. my mother's and/or father's expected time home.

0 1 2   2. what to do if my mother or father is late coming home from work.

0   1   2   3. to call and check in when I return
                    home from school.

0   1   2   4. to phone before I leave the house so
                    that someone knows where I am
                    going and when I will return home.

0   1   2   5. adults to call in an emergency if I
                    cannot contact my parents.

0   1   2   6. friends' or neighbors' homes to go
                    to if I am frightened or lonely.

0   1   2   7. ways to keep myself occupied in the
                    afternoon.

0   1   2   8. how to act if there is a strange noise
                    in the house.

0   1   2   9. what to do if I'm cut and bleeding.

0   1   2   10. what to do if I'm burned.

0   1   2   11. what to do if I have a headache or
                    stomachache.

0   1   2   12. to always speak with a parent,
                    responsible adult, or physician before
                    I take any medication.

0   1   2   13. the safe use of cooking and other
                    appliances.

0   1   2   14. how to effectively contact the police,
                    firefighters, or poison control center
                    in the event of an emergency.

0 1 2   15. what to do if I am followed by a stranger.

0 1 2   16. where to go if my keys are lost or misplaced.

0 1 2   17. what to do if I lose my money or transportation pass.

0 1 2   18. what to do when there is a call for a parent who is not at home.

0 1 2   19. not to tell a stranger on the phone that I am home alone.

0 1 2   20 to hang up if a caller is annoying or threatening.

0 1 2   21. what to say when an unknown person knocks at the door.

0 1 2   22. not to open the door for any strangers, no matter what they say or what uniform they wear.

0 1 2   23. the difference between "good" and "bad" touching.

0 1 2   24. what to do if I find an intruder in my home.

0 1 2   25. areas in the neighborhood that are considered safer, and the places to avoid.

SCORE

45–50   Congratulations! You and your child

have worked hard. Your youngster knows how to maturely respond to a variety of situations encountered when home alone.

40–45   You are on your way. Your child is able to demonstrate some readiness skills. With extra help in reviewing those areas that posed some problems, your youngster will be more prepared to be in an unsupervised setting.

40 or below   Your child is not yet able to be home without supervision. There is still much to learn. Please go back and reread those sections that are unfamiliar to your youngster. With patience and understanding, your child will eventually be ready to be home alone.

Communication Scale

Most working mothers and fathers work hard at being good parents. This effort is crucial if children are to adjust to being unsupervised. In our research we have found that youngsters are more secure being home alone when their feelings are respected, family affection is freely shared, and their parents respond thoughtfully and lovingly to their concerns.

Even if your child scored well on the Readiness Scale

there are other essential elements to consider in judging whether your youngster is ready to be home alone. The Communication Scale enables you to determine how well attuned you and your child are to each other. The following questions are important to consider when evaluating your family's strengths.

1. Do you and your child enjoy telling each other "I love you?"

2. Is yours a family where affection is freely shown?

3. Do you generally speak to each other in a caring way?

4. When upset about something important, is your child usually able to tell you?

5. Do you set aside time to talk on a regular basis?

6. Do you like being with one another?

7. Are there special times set aside for family activities?

8. Do you share information regarding personal family concerns?

9. Are you able to offer praise freely?

10. Do you try to quickly resolve differences after an argument?

11. Do you encourage your child to bring friends home?

12. Does your child become particularly stressed in new situations?

13. If being home alone proves to too difficult for your child, are you willing to make other arrangements?

SCORE

Think about your responses. Weigh your answers carefully. Those of you who were able to answer most of the questions with a strong affirmative reply obviously have a close relationship. You are aware of the significance of being sensitive to your child's needs at home and on the job.

For others, trying to combine the dual demands of working and parenting can leave you depleted. Being a working parent can be tough. But being home alone can be difficult, too. All children need to feel that their mothers and fathers want to and will be caring and supportive. Being emotionally "tuned in" provides the foundation that allows kids the strength to venture forth into new challenges and growing experiences.

Child's Thoughts

We hope that this section on children's thoughts will give you another opportunity to think about and voice any remaining anxieties concerning possibilities that could lie ahead.

I think I would be comfortable being home alone: (circle your answer)

Always

Sometimes

Never

I want to stay home alone _____ days each week. (circle your answer)

One

Two

Three

Four

Five

None

I want to stay by myself _____ hours each day. (circle your answer)

Up to one half hour

Up to one hour

One to two hours

More than two hours

I am looking forward to being on my own because

_____

_____

_____

What worries me the most about being on my own is:

_____

_____

_____

I would feel safer being by myself if:

_____

_____

_____

Mother's and/or Father's Work Numbers

It is important to have your mother's and father's work numbers and the list of emergency phone numbers posted in a convenient place, so that they are always available when you need them.

Mother's workplace_____

Address_____

Telephone number_____extension_____

Best time to call my mom _____

Time when my mom usually calls me _____

Father's workplace _____

Address _____

Telephone number _____ extension _____

Best time to call my dad _____

Time when my dad usually calls me _____

Emergency Phone Numbers

(To be posted by the telephone)

Your name _____

Address _____

Telephone _____

Police/emeregency _____

Police/information _____

Fire/emergency _____

Fire/information _____

Poison Control Center _____

Print the person's name on the first line.
Print the telephone number on the following line.

1. Neighbor, friend _____

_____

2. Neighbor, friend _____

_____

3. Relative _____

_____

4. Relative _____

_____

5. School _____

_____

6. Pediatrician _____

_____

7. Dentist _____

_____

8. Family Clinic _____

_____

9. Pharmacy _____

_____

10. Plumber _____

_____

11. Electrician _____

_____

12. Apartment manager _____

_____

13. Veterinarian _____

_____

14. Telephone company _____
15. Electric company _____
16. Gas/oil company _____
17. Taxi company _____

Legal Concerns

It is important for mothers and fathers to be aware that various states have laws relating to the safety and age of children home alone. To be advised of the child endangerment laws in your particular state, please contact the Department of Social Services, your state representative, or your state attorney general's office.

Acknowledgments

We wish to thank so many for their assistance in creating this book.

We are most grateful for the time, thought, and effort of the thousand schoolchildren across the country who responded to our Survey of Attitudes. Their reactions have enabled us to better understand what children need to be taught before they are ready to be home alone.

Hundreds of youngsters sat with us and allowed us to interview them. They candidly shared their feelings, fears, and ideas. Their personal stories of the struggles and strengths of being on their own are incorporated in the anecdotal material in this book.

Teachers and principals, concerned educators, spoke with us of the increasing number of working families and its impact on their students. They see children trying to adjust to new demands—some are well prepared, while others need emotional reassurance and advice.

The valuable and continuing contributions of many others in the study of the impact of children home alone enhanced our own research.

Rebecca Sweder typed the manuscript and made changes. She was able to sustain good cheer and enthusiasm as well as offer suggestions.

Our agent, Peter Ginsburg, believed in this project and in the need to help working parents and their children in a concrete, practical way.

Our editor, Margaret Zusky, made valuable suggestions, offered insightful observations, and added a fresh perspective to the work.

Netta Grollman has always given support and love to every effort and project, as she nurtures three delightful children, David, Sharon, and Jonathan, and six wonderful grandchildren.

Kenneth, Justin, and Rebecca Sweder freely offered thoughtful comments and encouragement, and as always they were a constant source of love and assistance during this undertaking and all others.

For our parents, Dorah and Gerson Grollman and Sylvia and Bert Gluck, and our parents-in-law, Rose and Sam Levinson and Edna and William Sweder, with us and with us in spirit, we have been blessed by their presence.

The affection and devotion of our other family and friends further sustains and rejuvenates us. We thank them all.

About the Authors

Earl A. Grollman, D.D., is a pioneer in the field of crisis intervention, and the author of twenty books, with over 500,000 in print. Among his works are *The Working Parent Dilemma* with Gerri L. Sweder, *Talking About Death: A Dialogue between Parent and Child,* and *Explaining Divorce to Children.* He writes regularly for *USA Today,* contributes to numerous professional and popular journals and magazines, and is an internationally acclaimed speaker and recipient of numerous awards, including the Distinguished Human Service Award from Yeshiva University. Rabbi Grollman also appears frequently on radio and television, including "Oprah Winfrey" and "Mr. Roger's Neighborhood." He is married and the father of three children.

Gerri L. Sweder, M.S.W., M.Ed., is a psychotherapist and family educator. Co-author with Earl A. Grollman of *The Working Parent Dilemma,* Mrs. Sweder is a child development and parenting specialist whose teaching experience has ranged from Head Start, high school, and graduate school. She appears on numerous radio and television programs, and was a regular commentator on the *Good Day* show

(Channel 5, Boston), addressing family concerns. She is the former co-president of the Boston Association for the Education of Young Children and a frequent speaker to parent and teacher associations and educational organizations. She received a B.S. degree from New York University, a master's degree in child studies from Wheelock College, and a master's in social work from Simmons College. She is married and the working mother of two adolescent children.

M